MW01629768

All about Advent & Christmas

"Catechetically rich and visually stunning, *All about Advent & Christmas* is just delightful! What a blessing to have such a thorough resource to use as a family during our favorite liturgical season, allowing us to dive even deeper into the meaning and traditions of these holy seasons. Children and adults alike will uncover new insights, as well as unique prayers and celebrations to incorporate into their liturgical life at home. I'll be returning to this lovely book every year!"

Katie Warner
Bestselling Catholic Children's Author, Creator of FirstFaithTreasury.com

"Take a deep dive into Advent with this all-encompassing guide. Katie breaks down topics in a way that is organized and simple for minds young and old to understand. This book will help prepare your heart for Christmas and should be a staple for every Catholic home. The stunning visuals are an added treat. Just lovely!"

Lindsay Trezza
Artist and Founder of Just Love Prints

"*All about Advent & Christmas* is all about the wonder, mystery, and joy of the gift of Jesus. It invites children and families on an adventurous ride through salvation history. As they go along the way, encountering the sights and wonders revealed in beautiful illustrations and clear, thorough catechesis, they will come to know deeply the story of God's own love for each one of us. It will be hard to open this book and not feel a sense of excitement about being Catholic and the coming celebration of the birth of our Lord within the first few pages."

Sr. Josephine Garrett, CSFN
Licensed Child and Adolescent Counselor

"To help your faith come alive, you need to live in tune with the liturgy. Katherine Bogner's *All about Advent & Christmas* helps us to do exactly that by unpacking the deeper meaning of our practices and leading us back to forgotten treasures. You won't regret picking up this beautifully written and illustrated book for your family."

R. Jared Staudt
Director of Content for Exodus 90

"Katherine Bogner has written yet another gorgeous guide to an important part of our Church's liturgical year. If you want to go beyond the Advent calendar and learn more about the fullness of the season, Katherine makes it so easy with this warm and inviting book."

Jenna Hines
Author of *The Lazy Liturgical*

"*All about Advent & Christmas* is small but mighty! Filled with vibrant illustrations and engaging explanations, this book will help converts and cradle Catholics alike better understand, appreciate, and more fully engage in the season of Advent. It's pretty enough to be a coffee table book and useful enough to be incorporated into a school unit on liturgical seasons—a great resource for individuals, families, and classrooms."

Bonnie Engstrom
Author of *Fulton Sheen and the Very Bad Week*

"This is not Katie's first book and I pray it's not her last! Once again she writes a book that is completely understandable for children but also offers new insights into what, why, and how to properly celebrate Advent. I, a priest, was reminded of or learned for the first time a few things while reading. If you have a child or you want to know more about Advent, I recommend this book to you!"

Fr. Eric Bolek
St. Mary of Lourdes Parish, Germantown Hills, IL

"With her trademark blend of deep insight and reverent wonder, Katie Bogner joyfully illuminates the path to the manger of Scripture and the manger of our hearts as we await the coming of the Light of the World."

Maura Roan McKeegan
Author of the Old and New series and *Julia Greeley, Secret Angel to the Poor*

"What a fantastic resource for families! The information is comprehensive yet easy to understand, and the artwork is beautiful. This is such a valuable tool to prepare our hearts and minds throughout Advent!"

Kate Frantz
Founder of Thy Olive Tree and Fiat Self-Publishing Academy

"*All about Advent & Christmas* is a great book that shares the history and traditions of the season of Advent with all of God's children. Miss Bogner touches upon the themes of Advent along with the major figures or saints of the season, which all point us to the Light in the Darkness, the Lamb of God, the Messiah who has come to save us, Our Lord Jesus Christ. As the secular world seems to rush to Christmas for a day, *All about Advent & Christmas* will help all God's children to better understand how we are called to prepare for the coming of the Messiah at Christmas!"

Fr. Michael Pica
Administrator of Immaculate Conception and St. John XXIII Parishes,
Catholic Diocese of Peoria

All about ADVENT & Christmas

*Sharing the Seasons of
Hope & Wonder with Children*

All about ADVENT & Christmas

Sharing the Seasons of Hope & Wonder with Children

By KATHERINE BOGNER

Illustrated & Designed by SHARI VAN VRANKEN

EMMAUS ROAD PUBLISHING

Steubenville, Ohio
www.emmausroad.org

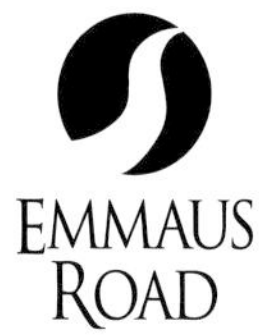

Emmaus Road Publishing
1468 Parkview Circle
Steubenville, Ohio 43952

Library of Congress Control Number: 2023945646
978-1-64585-345-9 Hardcover | 978-1-64585-347-3 Ebook

Design, layout and illustration by Shari Van Vranken

Nihil obstat:
Msgr. Philip D. Halfacre, V.G.
Censor Librorum

Imprimatur:
Most Rev. Louis Tylka
Bishop of Peoria

3 May 2023

The nihil obstat and imprimatur are declarations that a book or pamphlet
is free of doctrinal or moral error. There is no implication that those
who have granted the nihil obstat or imprimatur agree with the
contents, opinions, or statements expressed therein.

DEDICATION

For my students: past, present, and future. May your hearts always be filled with hope and the eager expectation of the Lord coming into your life!

In gratitude to our Lord Jesus Christ and to my family.

Brad, I love you. Thank you for your patience with me. I appreciate your hard work and the many sacrifices you make for our family.

Luke, you are my miracle and my joy. I love you. I pray you will always know how much God loves you and how much love and hope you bring to my life!

Mom and Dad, thank you for always encouraging me to use my gifts.

—SHARI

CONTENTS

Light and Darkness

When it is very, very dark, even a tiny glimmer of light helps our eyes navigate the darkness. Think of the night-light in your bedroom when you wake up to get a drink of water or the beam of a flashlight out in the yard while you play hide and seek.

Many years ago the flame of a candle or the burning wick of an oil lamp would have brightened the darkness in people's homes. And everywhere in every time, countless stars sparkle in the night sky and give us light to walk by. Light helps us feel hope even when it is very dark.

When God created the world, the first thing He did was speak light into being. God made the sun, moon, and stars to illuminate our journey and brighten both our days and nights. God declared the light to be good. By that light we can see in order to work and play. That same light warms the earth and helps plants grow. We are meant to be surrounded by light!

Waiting for the Coming of the Messiah

Our first parents, Adam and Eve, were created by God out of love. He loved them (and all their children, including you and me!) even when they didn't love Him back. They committed the original sin by not trusting God.

Choosing sin is like hiding in the dark, afraid and alone, even when God has promised us the gift of light. That first sin broke Adam and Eve's relationship with God, and they couldn't fix it on their own. But God the Father loved us so much that He promised to send a Messiah to save us!

Salvation History

We call the story of God's plan to save us "salvation history." The Bible records the people, places, and events of the past, each of which is connected to the others as part of a greater story.

Salvation history is also our story too. We can learn from the past and have a part in God's plan for all people. Salvation history is like a puzzle in which each of us is an irreplaceable piece.

After the Garden of Eden all of creation waited with longing for the Messiah, Our Savior, to come. The Messiah would save us from our sins and open the way to heaven, restoring our relationship with God the Father. But the Messiah didn't arrive after one year, or ten years, or even one hundred years. So God's people, the Israelites, continued to wait.

The Israelites understood the darkness of sin. They were stuck in a terrible cycle of turning away from God and then crying out for His help. But they were not without hope—God made covenants with them to show that He would keep His promise to send the Savior.

That's where Advent begins—it is a time of waiting for the coming Messiah. We wait in trust with Adam, Noah, Abraham, Isaac, Jacob, Moses, and David. We wait in hope with Eve, Sarah, Rebekah, Rachel, Judith, Esther, and Ruth.

And what were they waiting for?

The Light of the world to come.

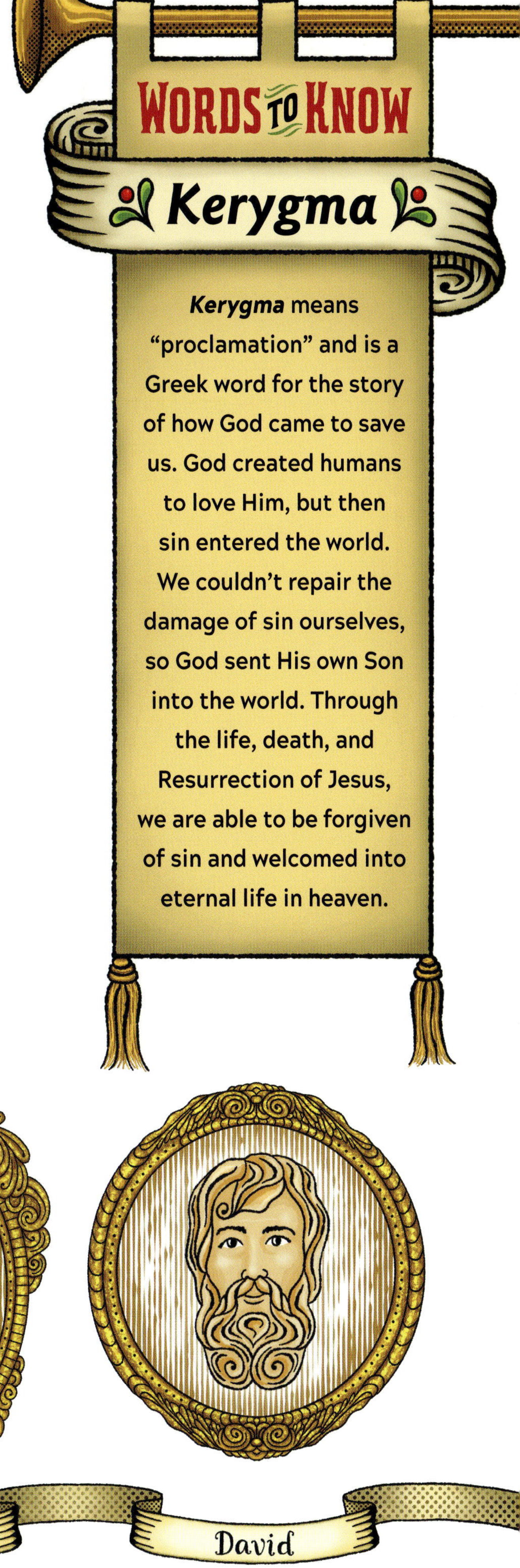

The **Liturgical Year**

From one generation to the next, God's people watched and waited for the coming Messiah. The Israelites had to wait for thousands of years for the Savior to come, but we already know the end of the story! God sent His only Son, Jesus, to be the Messiah.

We know that Jesus was born in Bethlehem and He grew up in the home of Mary and Joseph. We know that He spent three years teaching, healing, and ministering to people, while calling them to follow Him. We know that He loved both God and neighbor. We know that He died on the Cross, was buried in a tomb, and rose from the dead three days later. Then, He ascended to heaven where He sits at the right hand of the Father, and He entrusted His Church to the leadership of the Apostles, giving us the sacraments as signs and sources of His grace.

Advent

✠ The **First Sunday of Advent** is the beginning of the liturgical year

Christmas

✠ December 25: **Christmas Day**

✠ January 6 (or Sunday after January 1): **Epiphany of the Lord**

Ordinary Time

✠ Sunday after Epiphany: **The Baptism of the Lord**

Lent

✠ **Ash Wednesday** is the beginning of the six weeks of Lent

✠ **Palm Sunday** is the last Sunday of Lent & the beginning of Holy Week

Sacred Triduum

✠ **Holy Thursday**

✠ **Good Friday**

✠ **Easter Vigil**

Easter

✠ **Easter Sunday**

✠ **Ascension of the Lord**

✠ **Pentecost**

Ordinary Time

✠ The last Sunday of the liturgical year is **The Solemnity of Our Lord Jesus Christ, King of the Universe**

Liturgical Colors

The Church is filled with so much meaning that even the colors we use are symbolic.
Each liturgical season has its own colors with special meanings.

Advent & Lent	*purple*	*preparation, penance*
Gaudete Sunday & Laetare Sunday	*rose*	*joy*
Ordinary Time	*green*	*growth, new life*
Christmas & Easter	*white, gold*	*celebration, rejoicing*
Sacred Triduum	*red*	*sacrifice*

Each year we walk with the Church through the stories of Jesus's life, reliving and remembering His life, death, and Resurrection. The structure we follow is called the liturgical year. It follows the same pattern each year, broken into parts called seasons.

These liturgical seasons help us to pray and learn about a certain part of Jesus's life. Advent and Christmas are spent waiting for, and then celebrating, His birth.

Ordinary Time helps us to grow and learn from His teachings.

Lent invites us to pray and fast with Jesus in the desert, leading to the sacred *triduum* ("three days") during which we remember the events of Holy Week and His Crucifixion.

During Easter we rejoice in His Resurrection and the new life Jesus gives us.

According to the Catechism

"The Church, in the course of the year, unfolds the whole mystery of Christ from His Incarnation and Nativity through His Ascension, to Pentecost and the expectations of the blessed hope of the coming of the Lord."

CATECHISM OF THE CATHOLIC CHURCH, §1194

The rhythm of our liturgical year reminds us of patterns in the created world. Think of how things grow: a seed is planted, sprouts, blooms, and is harvested. With the harvest comes a time of celebration and rest and then the cycle starts over. Our God is a God of order! He gives us the structure of the liturgical year to help us grow closer to Him year after year.

"With today's first Sunday of Advent, a new liturgical year begins. The Church takes up her journey again, and invites us to reflect more intensely on the mystery of Christ, a mystery that is always new and that time cannot exhaust. Christ is the Alpha and the Omega, the beginning and the end. Thanks to him, the history of humanity proceeds as a pilgrimage toward the fulfillment of the Kingdom which He inaugurated with his Incarnation and victory over sin and death."

— POPE ST. JOHN PAUL II[1]

The Advent Season

> *"For yet a little while, and the coming one shall come and shall not tarry."*
>
> — HEBREWS 10:37

Even though we already know that God's promise of the Messiah was fulfilled in Jesus, we still wait with anticipation each year to celebrate His birth. This waiting is meant to open our hearts and fill them with hope, so we never forget how wonderful it is that Jesus came to save us.

Together with the whole Church, we wait and prepare for four weeks during the season of Advent at the beginning of each new liturgical year. Those four Sundays act as a countdown to the awaited celebration of Christmas, our Savior's birth. We spend Advent in joyful expectation of the coming of Christ.

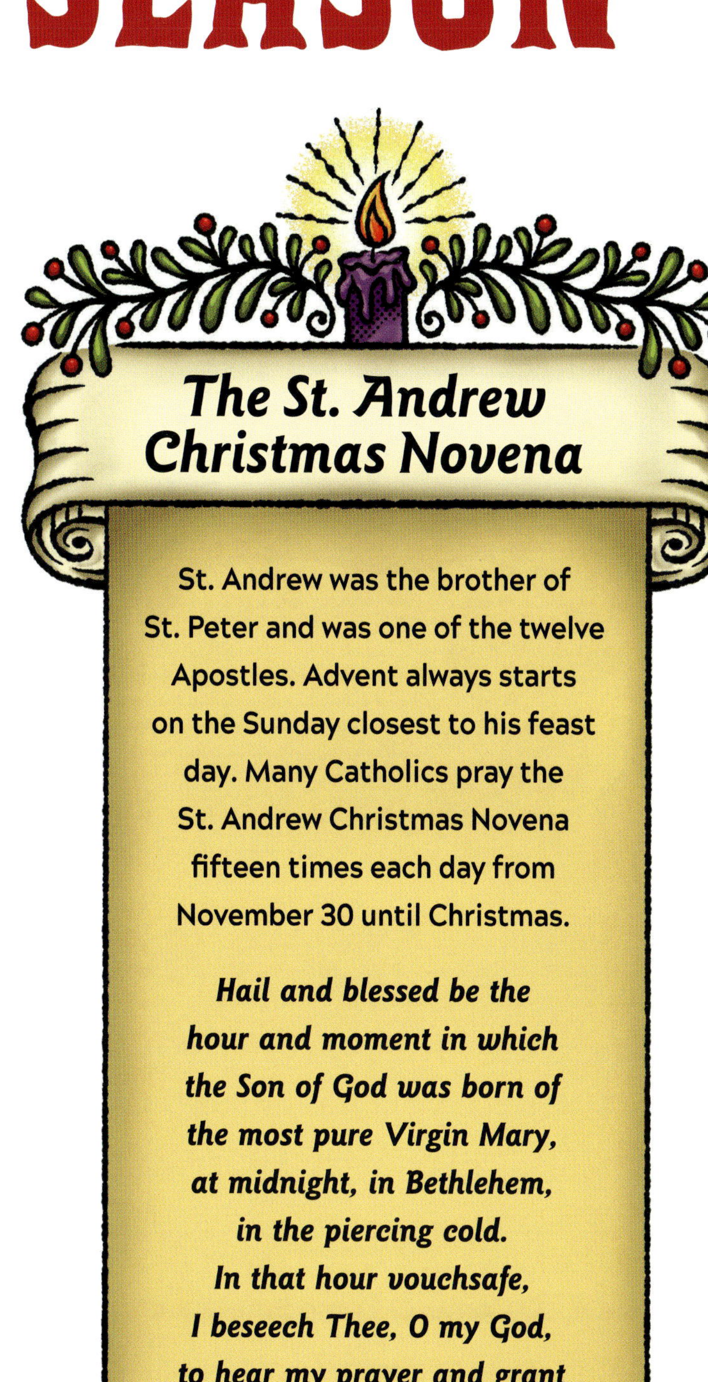

St. Andrew was the brother of St. Peter and was one of the twelve Apostles. Advent always starts on the Sunday closest to his feast day. Many Catholics pray the St. Andrew Christmas Novena fifteen times each day from November 30 until Christmas.

Hail and blessed be the hour and moment in which the Son of God was born of the most pure Virgin Mary, at midnight, in Bethlehem, in the piercing cold. In that hour vouchsafe, I beseech Thee, O my God, to hear my prayer and grant my desires through the merits of our Savior Jesus Christ, and of His blessed mother. Amen.

The word *advent* originates from Latin and means "to come." Each Advent, as we wait for Jesus to come, we can meditate on the past, present, and future. We remember the waiting throughout the whole Old Testament for the Messiah to come. We wait for this year's celebration of Christmas. And we also wait for Jesus to come again at the end of time, when He will create a new heaven and a new earth.

Just as Mary and Joseph must have been filled with wonder and awe when they looked into the face of their infant Savior, we wait with hope during Advent and look forward to the day when we will see Him face to face!

Advent Hymns

You probably can sing along to many Christmas songs, but did you know that there are also beautiful hymns that are perfect for the season of Advent?

The words and melodies of these songs help us to understand the longing of the Israelites as they awaited the Messiah. These songs also help us to meditate on the coming of Christmas.

* O Come, O Come Emmanuel
* *Alma Redemptoris Mater*
* Come, Thou Long Expected Jesus
* In the Bleak Midwinter
* The King Shall Come
* The Coming of Our Lord
* Let All Mortal Flesh Keep Silence

* Lift Up Your Heads, You Mighty Gates
* On Jordan's Bank
* O Come, Divine Messiah
* The Advent of Our King
* People, Look East
* The Angel Gabriel from Heaven Came
* Lo, How a Rose E'er Blooming

The ADVENT WREATH

"The people who walked in darkness have seen a great light; those who dwelt in a land of deep darkness, on them has light shined."

— ISAIAH 9:2

There are many traditions associated with Advent, but one of the most recognizable is the Advent wreath. Although it originated in Germany and Scandinavia, the wreath has grown to become quite popular in North America. The Advent wreath is filled with symbolism that teaches us about the season of Advent.

The wreath's evergreen branches remind us of the everlasting life we have through Christ.

The circular shape tells us that the Lord has no beginning or end.

Four candles are used to mark the four weeks, and the burning of their wicks help bring light to the darkness.

As the candles burn down, they mark the passing of time, reminding us of the long waiting of God's people for the coming Messiah.

While Advent wreaths have been used in homes for hundreds of years, they recently became a part of the liturgy. The Advent wreath in a church is blessed on the first Sunday of Advent by the priest and a new candle is lit each week until Christmas. Both at Mass and at home, the Advent wreath helps us to keep the coming of the Light of the world at the center of our prayer during the season of Advent.

Hope, Peace, Joy, Love

Advent candles aren't just pretty–they have meanings that match the weekly readings from Mass! The candles stand for hope, peace, joy, and love. We work to grow in these virtues to be better able to welcome the Infant Savior and to spread His light in the world.

First Week of Advent  HOPE

Second Week of Advent  PEACE

Third Week of Advent  JOY

Fourth Week of Advent  LOVE

Pray Together: The Advent Wreath

- Set up your Advent wreath in a central location, like the dinner table. Light the candles while gathered for family meals or during prayer before bed.

- Pray an Advent wreath blessing prayer on the first Sunday of Advent, such as the one shared on the United States Conference of Catholic Bishops (USCCB) website.

- Read a Scripture selection from the Mass readings and sing "O Come, O Come Emmanuel" as you light the candles.

- Share family prayer intentions and thanksgivings.

PURPLE

The liturgical color violet (or purple) doesn't just remind us of royalty; it also reminds us of preparation, sacrifice, and the Sacrament of Confession.

In addition to being the color for the season of Advent, it is also the color for the season of Lent.

While most parishes will use the same purple vestments and liturgical articles, sometimes a blue-violet color is used for Advent and a red-violet color is used for Lent. One reason for this is because of the Advent season's close connection with the Blessed Virgin Mary, whose traditional color is blue. The red used during the Lenten season reminds us of Jesus's Blood and His death on Good Friday.

Some Advent wreaths hold four white candles, as the earliest Advent wreaths traditionally did, but most modern Catholic Advent wreaths include candles that match the liturgical colors of the season. The three purple candles remind us of the royalty of the coming Messiah. The rose candle, lit on the third Sunday, represents the joy we feel as Christmas nears. A fifth white candle, called the Christ Candle, can be placed in the center of the wreath and lit during the Octave of Christmas.

Advent Traditions Around the World

While the Advent wreath is likely the most recognizable Advent tradition in North America and many European countries, it certainly isn't the only way that Christians get ready for the coming of Jesus. All around the world different Advent traditions are used to prepare the hearts of the people for the celebration of Christmas.

In Eastern European countries like Poland and Hungary, it is customary to attend an early morning Mass each day of Advent. The Byzantine Catholic Church and other Eastern rites have the Nativity fast, a forty-day period of fasting which lasts from mid-November until Christmas. Eastern Catholic rites also place a special emphasis on the Blessed Virgin Mary during Advent with a series of Marian feasts leading up to Christmas, which serve as a reminder that every celebration of Mary is always a celebration of Christ!

According to the Catechism

"When the Church celebrates the liturgy of Advent each year, she makes present this ancient expectancy of the Messiah, for by sharing in the long preparation for the Savior's first coming, the faithful renew their ardent desire for his second coming."

THE CATECHISM OF THE CATHOLIC CHURCH, §524

Bambinelli (Baby Jesus) Sunday in Italy takes place on the third Sunday of Advent. Families bring the Baby Jesus figurine from their Nativity sets to church to have them blessed in preparation for Christmas. Pope St. Paul VI even made it a custom for this event to take place in the Vatican. Pilgrims can have their Baby Jesus statue blessed by the pope himself!

Straw for Baby Jesus

Another activity that can be done during Advent focuses on growing in virtue each day. Before they set up their Nativity scene figurines, some families have a special spot for the empty manger. Throughout Advent, whenever someone says an extra prayer or does a good deed, they place a piece of straw or yarn in the manger, helping to make a warm bed for Baby Jesus.

In Latin American countries like Mexico and Guatemala, a festival called *Las Posadas* (which means "the inns") begins on December 16 and lasts for nine days. A group of people led by children playing the roles of an angel, Joseph, and Mary travels to a different home or church each night. They sing carols and read Bible stories along the way, but often are turned away by the hosts because there is "no room at the inn." On Christmas Eve they are finally welcomed inside the church and celebrate with Mass and special treats.

Advent Calendars

Advent calendars, often filled with chocolates, scenes from a story, or other small treats, are a fun way that Catholics around the world count down the coming of Christmas with a surprise for each day of Advent. They help remind us of the anticipation of waiting for Jesus to come!

"At this Christmas when Christ comes, will He find a warm heart? Mark the season of Advent by loving and serving the others with God's own love and concern."

— ST. TERESA OF CALCUTTA[2]

The JESSE ✳ TREE

"There shall come forth a shoot from the stump of Jesse,
and a branch shall grow out of his roots.
And the Spirit of the LORD shall rest upon him,
the spirit of wisdom and understanding,
the spirit of counsel and might,
the spirit of knowledge
and the fear of the LORD."
— ISAIAH 11:1–2

Advent is a season of anticipation, but it is also a season of memory. We remember the long years of waiting as the people of God watched and hoped for the Messiah. In the Old Testament, we read the stories of those men and women. One Advent tradition is to learn about and pray with the people from the family into which Jesus would be born.

The prophet Isaiah wrote about a "branch" that would come from Jesse's family tree (Isa 11). That branch would be the Messiah, and He would bring about the kingdom of God. You might not know much about Jesse, but you probably have heard about his son David, the shepherd boy who defeated the giant Goliath and one day became the king of Israel. Jesus is called the Son of David in the Gospels, which highlights the belief that He fulfilled the word of the prophets.

If you've ever read the beginning of the Gospel of Matthew, you know that it starts with a long list of names. While it would be easy to just speed past them, those names are important! This is the genealogy of Jesus, and it tells us about the family into which He was born. Open up your Bible to Matthew 1:1-17 and see if you recognize any of their names. Do you know how these men and women fit into the story of the coming of Jesus?

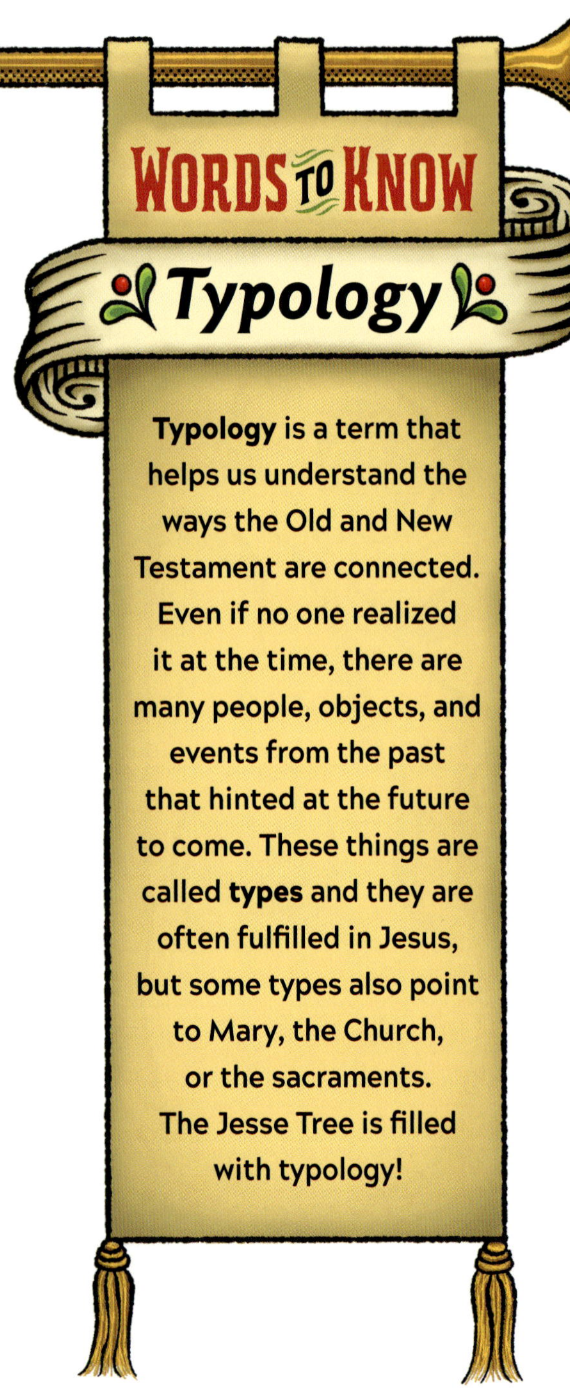

Typology is a term that helps us understand the ways the Old and New Testament are connected. Even if no one realized it at the time, there are many people, objects, and events from the past that hinted at the future to come. These things are called **types** and they are often fulfilled in Jesus, but some types also point to Mary, the Church, or the sacraments. The Jesse Tree is filled with typology!

The Jesse Tree is an Advent tradition that teaches us the stories of the ancestors of Jesus. Starting with Adam and moving through the whole Old Testament, a different person in the bloodline of the Messiah is remembered each day of Advent by reading a passage from Scripture.

A set of ornaments with symbols for each person can go along with the Bible stories, and one ornament can be added to a Christmas tree or a garland each day as Christmas draws near.

The Jesse Tree helps us to remember those who waited with hope for the coming Messiah.

The BLESSED VIRGIN MARY

If we fast-forward through the generations in Jesus's family tree, we meet Joseph and Mary. They knew the prophecies about the coming Savior, and God called them to play a pivotal role in His story.

Mary was set apart and prepared to be the mother of the Messiah. She was pure and holy, filled with grace, and had a heart completely in tune with God's will.

The Lord sent the Archangel Gabriel to announce that the moment that all of creation had been waiting for had finally arrived! God would send the Savior, His Son Jesus, into the world to save us from our sins, and He asked Mary to be His mother. She responded, "Let it be to me according to your word" (Luke 1:38).

The Annunciation

While we actually celebrate the Solemnity of the Annunciation on March 25, Advent is still a perfect time to think about the Annunciation. Mary's "Yes!" to God's question, carried by the Archangel Gabriel, brought Jesus into the world. During the waiting period of Advent, the whole Church meditates on the nine months that Mary waited for Jesus to be born. You can read about the Annunciation in Luke 1:26-38.

Mary's Magnificat

My soul proclaims the
greatness of the Lord,

my spirit rejoices in God my
Savior for he has looked with
favor on his lowly servant.

From this day all generations
will call me blessed:

the Almighty has done
great things for me,
and holy is his Name.

He has mercy on those who
fear him in every generation.

He has shown the
strength of his arm,

he has scattered the
proud in their conceit.

He has cast down the
mighty from their thrones,

and has lifted up the lowly.

He has filled the hungry
with good things,

and the rich he has
sent away empty.

He has come to the help
of his servant Israel

for he has remembered
his promise of mercy,

the promise he made to
our fathers, to Abraham and
his children forever.
Amen.

BASED ON LUKE 1:46–55

What wonder and awe she must have felt to know that God's promises were being fulfilled with her *fiat*, her yes. Imagine the nine months Mary waited like a living tabernacle with Jesus growing within her. Mary knew that hidden in her womb was the Light of the world.

Advent is a beautiful time to come to know the Blessed Virgin Mary more deeply! Try asking her to help you to love Jesus more each day.

Mary didn't just care for Jesus when He was a baby. She was the first and most perfect disciple, and she followed Jesus even to the foot of the Cross. After Jesus ascended back to heaven, Mary stayed with the early Church and was present at the descent of the Holy Spirit at Pentecost.

Jesus shares Mary with us, giving us a spiritual mother to pray for us and guide us.

What a gift we have in Mary, the Mother of God, who is also a mother to us all.

Celebrating the Immaculate Conception

The Solemnity of the Immaculate Conception honors Mary and reminds us that she was free from all sin from the very moment of her conception and remained sinless her entire life. This feast reminds us to look to Mary as a model of purity, grace, and obedience to the will of God.

- **Feast day: December 8**

- **Plan a meal with all white food to symbolize Mary's Immaculate Conception and sinless life. (For example—chicken, pasta with alfredo sauce, cheesecake, vanilla ice cream, and white grape juice!)**

- **Go to Mass—it's a holy day of obligation!**

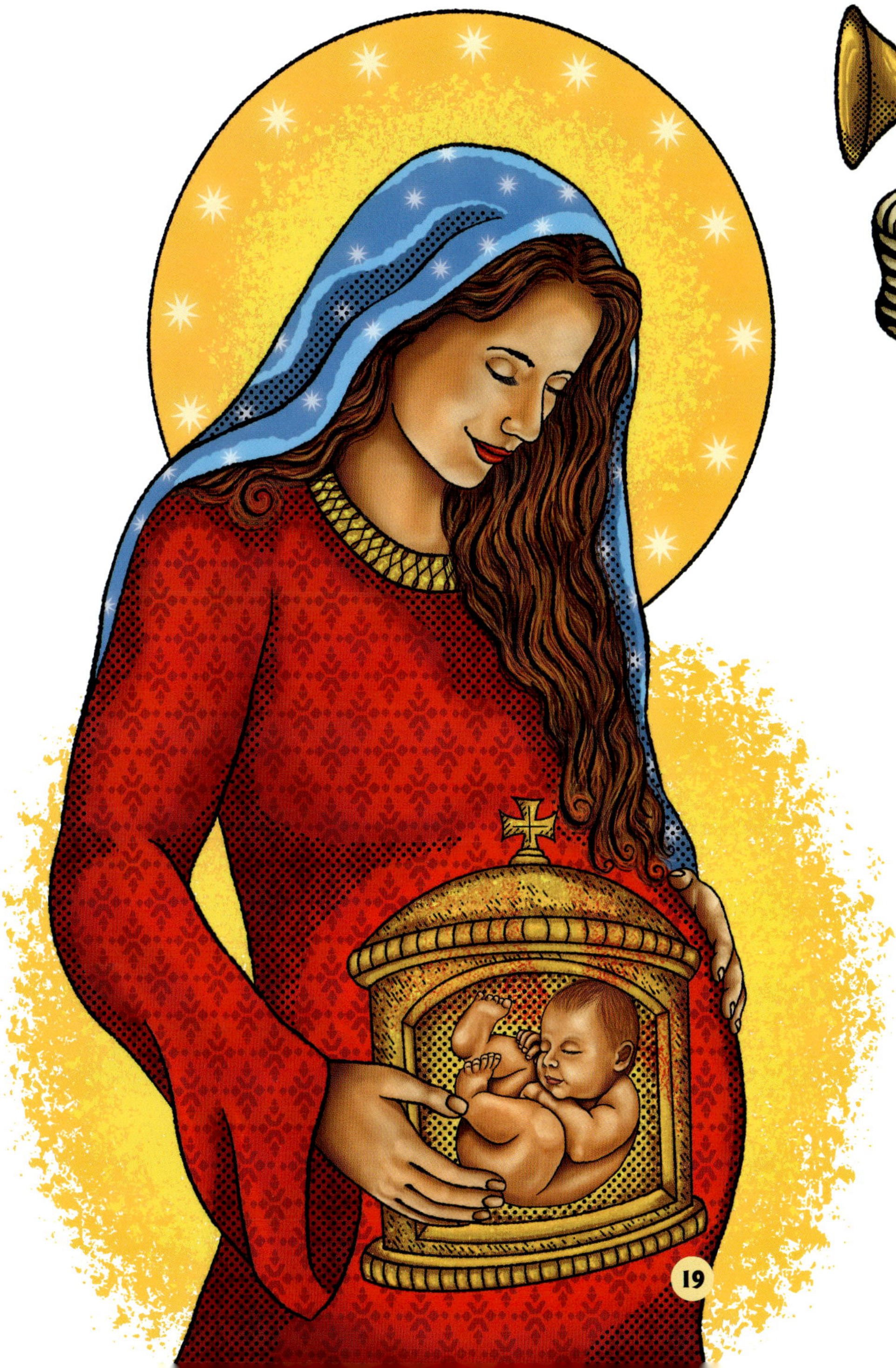

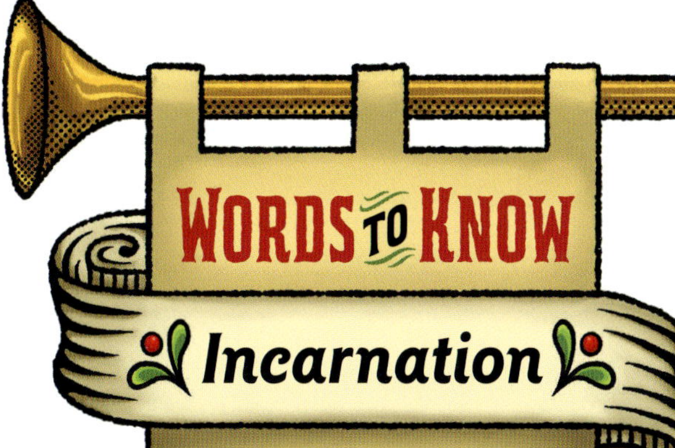

The **Incarnation** is the truth that God became Man in the person of Jesus Christ. Jesus is fully God and fully man. This is called a mystery of our faith because it is something that we believe but cannot fully explain or understand.

The Incarnation occurred in the womb of the Blessed Virgin Mary at the Annunciation, but we also celebrate the Incarnation in a special way each Christmas.

Advent is a perfect time to ponder the mystery and wonder of the Incarnation!

SAINT JOSEPH

> *And Joseph also went up from Galilee, from the city of Nazareth, to Judea, to the city of David, which is called Bethlehem, because he was of the house and lineage of David, to be enrolled with Mary his betrothed, who was with child. And while they were there, the time came for her to be delivered. And she gave birth to her first-born son and wrapped him in swaddling cloths, and laid him in a manger, because there was no place for them in the inn.*
>
> **— LUKE 2:4–7**

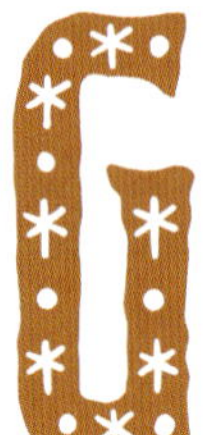

God never does anything without great preparation. Just as He chose Mary to be the mother of Jesus, He prepared St. Joseph to be the adoptive father who would care for Jesus here on earth.

Joseph was righteous and holy, virtuous and just. He was a hard worker who could protect and provide for the Holy Family.

God's plan for Joseph to take Mary as his wife was revealed to Joseph through a dream. He listened and immediately obeyed.

St. Joseph has several other dreams recorded in the Gospels, and each of them show his trust and willingness to follow God. From Bethlehem to Egypt, and from Nazareth to Jerusalem, Joseph was ready to lead Mary and Jesus wherever God called them to go.

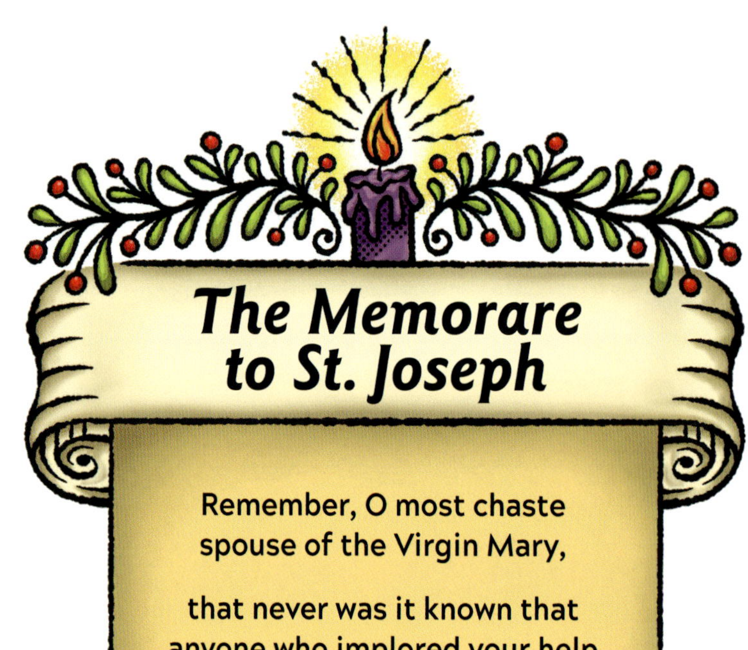

Mary and Joseph knew the stories of the Old Testament. They understood that their people had been waiting for the promises of God to be fulfilled. Joseph was of the family of David, from whom the Messiah would come. And now he and Mary would be the ones to welcome Him into the world.

It was revealed to both Mary and Joseph that the name they would give the Messiah would be Jesus. How amazing that God, Who had been known as the great "I AM" in the Old Testament, would now have a familiar and comforting name, the name of Jesus, which means "God saves!"

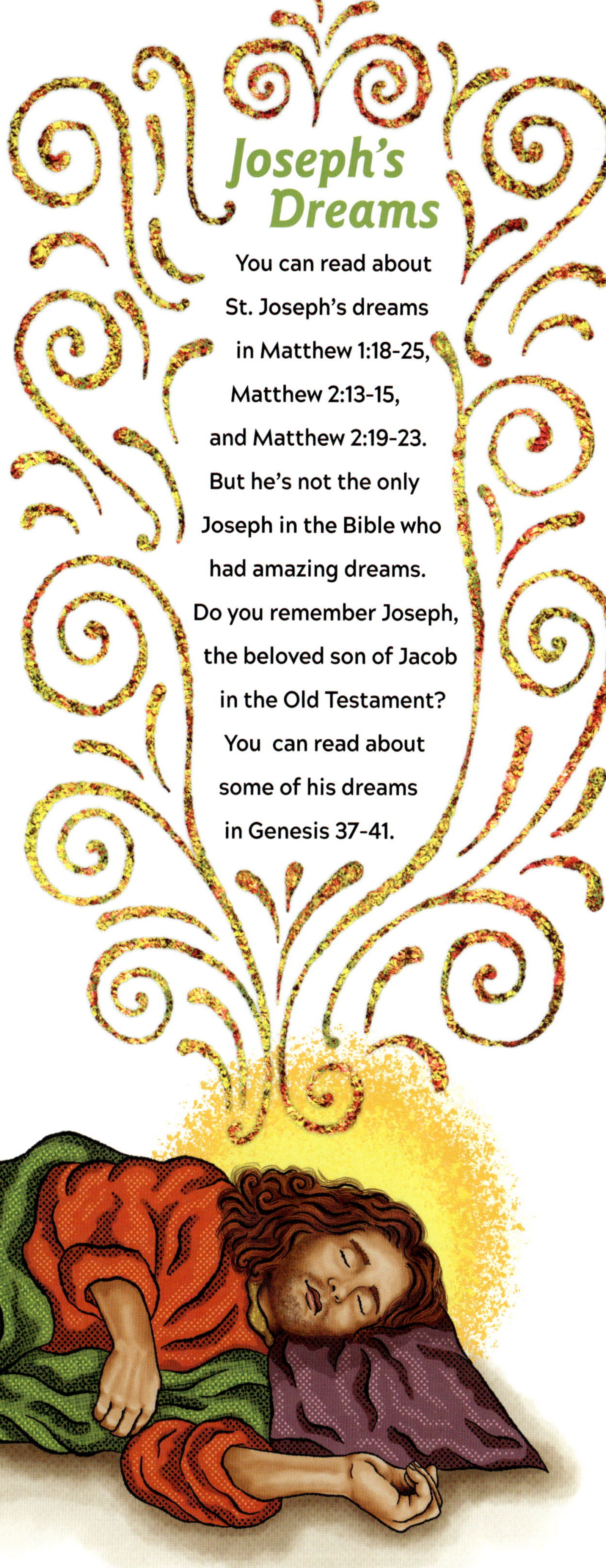

Joseph's Dreams

You can read about St. Joseph's dreams in Matthew 1:18-25, Matthew 2:13-15, and Matthew 2:19-23. But he's not the only Joseph in the Bible who had amazing dreams. Do you remember Joseph, the beloved son of Jacob in the Old Testament? You can read about some of his dreams in Genesis 37-41.

Saint John the Baptist

While the Blessed Virgin Mary was awaiting the birth of Jesus, she went to visit another miraculous baby. At the Annunciation, Gabriel had told Mary that her cousin Elizabeth was also expecting a baby. Elizabeth and her husband Zechariah had been unable to have a child even though they had been married for many years.

The Archangel Gabriel had also visited Zechariah to announce the coming of their son, John. He told Zechariah that John would go before the Lord to prepare the hearts of the people for His coming.

When Mary arrived at the home of Zechariah and Elizabeth, baby John leapt in Elizabeth's womb. Filled with the Holy Spirit even as a baby, John recognized the Savior!

Archbishop Fulton J. Sheen wrote, "All the longings and expectations of thousands of years as to Him Who would be the Savior are now fulfilled in this one ecstatic moment when John the Baptist greets Christ, the Son of the Living God."[3]

Did You Know?

Even the natural world can point us to the truth of the Bible. The feast of the Nativity of John the Baptist is on June 24.

In the Northern Hemisphere, the amount of light each day gets shorter and shorter for six months after his feast day.

Then in December just before Christmas Eve, the days begin to get longer and longer. Just as John said that he must decrease so that Jesus could increase, the length of sunlight of each day reminds us of John's preparation for Jesus to come as the Light of the world.

St. John the Baptist has a leading role in the
readings for both Advent and Lent.

During Advent we hear him call us to make
way for the Lord in our hearts. During Lent,
John calls for repentance from sin.

John fulfilled the words of the prophet Isaiah:

"A voice cries:

'In the wilderness prepare the way of the Lord,
make straight in the desert a highway for our God.

Every valley shall be lifted up,
and every mountain and hill be made low;
the uneven ground shall become level,
and the rough places a plain.'"

— ISAIAH 40:3–4

John grew up and began proclaiming the good news about the Messiah. He went into the wilderness and many people came to hear him teach.

John invited the people to convert, challenging them to turn their hearts toward God. One day, Jesus Himself came to John to be baptized, marking the beginning of Jesus's public ministry.

One of John the Baptist's best known quotes in Scripture is "He must increase, but I must decrease" (John 3:30). John, the voice crying out in the wilderness, was a prophet who pointed the way. But now that it was time for Jesus to shine in the world, John stepped back and encouraged the people to follow Jesus.

During Advent, John the Baptist reminds us to watch and prepare for Jesus's arrival while we share the good news with others.

SAINTS of ADVENT

 ary, Joseph, Elizabeth, Zechariah, and John aren't the only saints who can help us draw closer to Jesus during the month of December.

Advent is peppered with the feast days of many holy men and women. Saints Nicholas, Juan Diego, and Lucy are a few beloved saints who are often celebrated in homes around the world while we are still preparing for Christmas.

We can learn from their stories and model their virtues. Their lives were changed by Jesus, and ours can be too!

December Feast Days

3   *St. Francis Xavier*

4   *St. John Damascene*

6   *St. Nicholas*

7   *St. Ambrose*

8   *Solemnity of the Immaculate Conception*

9   *St. Juan Diego*

12   *Our Lady of Guadalupe*

13   *St. Lucy*

14   *St. John of the Cross*

21   *St. Peter Canisius*

23   *St. John of Kanty*

25   *Solemnity of the Nativity of the Lord*

26   *St. Stephen*

27   *St. John the Apostle*

28   *The Holy Innocents*

29   *St. Thomas Becket*

30   *Holy Family (or Sunday after Christmas)*

31   *St. Sylvester I*

St. Nicholas

St. Nicholas was a bishop in third-century Turkey. He is remembered for helping the poor and sick. The most well-known story of St. Nicholas is about him secretly leaving money for the three daughters of a poor man to provide dowries for them. He threw bags of gold coins in the window of their home and the coins landed in the girls' stockings, which were hung by the fire to dry. The real St. Nicholas is the origin of various Santa Claus traditions around the world.

Celebrating St. Nicholas

Feast day: December 6

Exchange Christmas stockings

Leave gold chocolate coins (like the money he gave) or candy canes (like his bishop's crosier) in the shoes of your loved ones

Make a donation to a charity of your choice

St. Lucy

St. Lucy, whose name means "light," was a third-century Christian martyr who is remembered for her charity to the poor. Also called St. Lucia, she is celebrated in several cultures on her feast day by having the youngest girl in the family serve sweet rolls by candlelight to family members while they are still in bed, reminding us of the way St. Lucy brought food to the poor under the cover of darkness.

Celebrating St. Lucy

Feast day: December 13

Make sweet rolls for breakfast or have breakfast in bed

Work or eat by candlelight

Drive around and look at the Christmas lights in your neighborhood

Drop off canned goods to your local food pantry

St. Juan Diego was a convert from Mexico who lived in the 1500s. Mary appeared to him and asked for a church to be built on the site where she visited him. As a sign of her request, beautiful roses appeared on the hill even though it was December. Juan gathered them up in his tilma (cloak) to take to the local bishop. When he opened the tilma to reveal the roses, an image of Mary, now known as Our Lady of Guadalupe, was miraculously imprinted on the fabric. This miracle led to the conversion of thousands. Our Lady of Guadalupe, now one of the most popular Marian images, is Patroness of the Americas.

Celebrating St. Juan Diego and Our Lady of Guadalupe

Feast days:
December 9 and December 12

—

Enjoy traditional Mexican food for dinner

—

Decorate your home with roses (you can use real flowers or draw your own pictures of roses)

—

Listen to a recording of a traditional Catholic prayer in Spanish

DECORATIONS *and* CELEBRATIONS

From the very creation of the world to the promises of the patriarchs through the words of the prophets, all throughout salvation history we see small steps leading toward the coming of the Messiah. Starting at the very beginning of time, God had been preparing for the coming of the Messiah into the world. If God can so lavishly prepare the world for Jesus, how important it must be for us to take the time to prepare both our hearts and homes during the four weeks of Advent!

Homes and churches are often decorated with greenery during Advent and Christmas. It looks beautiful, smells wonderful, and is also filled with symbolism about Christ!

SACRAMENT CONNECTION:
Confession

The Christmas season is usually very busy. It's filled with delicious meals and sweet treats, guests, and parties to attend! Before all the baking and decorating begins, we often take some time to clean our homes to prepare for the Christmas decorations.

We can do the same for our souls. Before the celebration of Christmas arrives, we should make time to examine our conscience and think about putting God first in our lives. If you are old enough, ask your family to help you receive the Sacrament of Confession at least once this Advent to help your soul be ready to receive Jesus at Christmas!

Evergreen wreaths and garlands, mistletoe, and ivy all remain green even in winter. They have come to represent the everlasting life we receive through Jesus.

Christmas trees, in addition to being evergreens, can remind us of the Tree of Life in the Garden of Eden as well as the Cross on which Jesus died.

Holly, with its pointy leaves and red berries, symbolizes Jesus's crown of thorns and drops of blood.

Christmas lights and candles remind us of Jesus being the Light of the world. A Nativity scene helps us to keep our focus on the reason for the season, the birth of Jesus in Bethlehem.

History of the Nativity Scene

St. Francis of Assisi is credited with creating the first Nativity scene (also called a créche). Gathering figurines of the Holy Family, shepherds, wise men, angels, and animals reminds us in our waiting during Advent to keep the true meaning of Christmas close to our hearts. Here are some ideas for being intentional with your Nativity scene this Advent:

- Set up your stable early in Advent and then slowly add more of the Nativity figurines each week.

- Wait to add Baby Jesus until Christmas Day!

- Have the wise men figurines "wander" through your home during the Christmas season as they look for Jesus. Add them to the Nativity on Epiphany.

As Christmas draws closer, we might get excited about receiving gifts from our family and friends. Most people exchange presents on Christmas to celebrate Jesus's birthday, but others receive surprises earlier on St. Nicholas's feast day or wait until Epiphany to give gifts like the magi did. No matter when you unwrap your Christmas presents, just remember that the reason that we give gifts is in celebration of the most important gift of the season, the birth of Jesus! Use this tradition of gift-giving to grow in the virtues of generosity and gratitude, and think of ways to consider the needs of others.

You don't have to rush to get all the decor up the first week of Advent. One way to experience the slow preparation of the season is to slowly add decorations throughout all of Advent. Our churches, for example, are not decorated during Advent; the lights and trees and flowers make their debut at the Christmas Vigil Mass and remain up until the feast of the Baptism of the Lord in January. However you choose to decorate your home, let the special decorations be a part of your preparation, helping to build up your excitement for the coming celebration of Christmas.

Celebrating the Twelve Days of Christmas

You may have heard of the Twelve Days of Christmas, but did you know that they are not a countdown? Rather, they are twelve days of celebration that begin on Christmas Day and last until the Solemnity of the Epiphany on January 6th.

There is an old English folk song called the Twelve Days of Christmas about receiving a set of unusual gifts. We can find hidden symbolism in the gifts to remind us of important truths of our faith. For example, the partridge in the pear tree represents Jesus on the Cross, the two turtle doves are the Old and New Testaments of the Bible, and the three French hens are the theological virtues of faith, hope, and love. Can you think of what the gifts on days four through twelve might symbolize?

GAUDETE ✠ SUNDAY

uring Advent we use the color purple to remind ourselves of preparing for Jesus to come at Christmas. But on the third Sunday of Advent, you might have a little surprise when you come to Mass and see the priest wearing pink!

Pink, or rose, is a color of joy. On the third Sunday of Advent we are over halfway through the season and drawing closer to the celebration of Christmas. We rejoice because our waiting is almost over!

Why Do We Use Latin?

Since the fourth century, Latin has been used as the language of prayer for the Catholic Church. United together, believers from around the world worship with one voice in the same language. While it is now more common for the prayers at Mass to be said in the local language, we still share beautiful Latin prayers, hymns, and liturgical terms, like Gaudete. Using Latin helps remind us that our Church is one, holy, catholic, and apostolic, and that our faith is for all people of all times. This Advent you could try learning a favorite prayer or hymn in Latin!

LAETARE SUNDAY

The season of Lent has its own pink Sunday. The fourth week of Lent begins with Laetare Sunday. *Laetare* means "to rejoice!" The word is taken from Isaiah 66:10, which begins "Rejoice with Jerusalem, and be glad for her, all you who love her." Like Gaudete Sunday, Laetare Sunday means that we are over halfway through the season of Lent. We rejoice because the joy of celebrating Jesus's Resurrection is near!

The third Sunday of Advent even has a special name; it is called Gaudete (pronounced gow-DAY-tay) Sunday. *Gaudete* is from Latin and, like *laetare*, also means "to rejoice." It is the first word of the entrance antiphon for Mass on Gaudete Sunday, and the readings that day are all about joy.

You may have noticed that there is no Gloria sung during Advent at the beginning of Mass. The Gloria is a prayer of joy, so we don't sing it again until we celebrate the birth of Jesus at Mass on Christmas. Then we rejoice with all the angels and saints that Jesus has come! Jesus came into the world as a baby that first Christmas, but he also comes to us each Mass in the Holy Eucharist. We are filled with joy that our Lord shares the gift of his Body and Blood with us!

he first reading is from either Isaiah or Zephaniah. Isaiah tells us to "greatly rejoice in the LORD" (61:10) and Zephaniah says to "rejoice and exult with all your heart" (3:14).

When we hear that "the wilderness and the dry land shall be glad, the desert shall rejoice and blossom" (Isa 35:1–2), we are reminded that the Lord can take the brokenness of the world and make it whole again. No sin is too big to be forgiven. We rejoice in the Lord who is so good to us.

The Joyful Mysteries

This week is a perfect time to pray the Joyful Mysteries of the Rosary, which tell the stories of Jesus's birth.

1

The Annunciation

2

The Visitation

3

The Nativity

4

The Presentation in the Temple

5

The Finding in the Temple

The Joyful Mysteries are all moments from Jesus's life that were filled with joy.

The O Antiphons

The O Antiphons are traditional, scriptural prayers we pray during the week leading up to Christmas Eve. These antiphons are like a countdown as we near the end of our waiting and our excitement grows. Jesus is almost here!

An antiphon is a short prayer that is spoken, sung, or chanted before and after a longer prayer. The O Antiphons feature the seven titles of the Messiah found in the Book of Isaiah. Each of the meanings of the names originally found in the Old Testament all match up to who Jesus was, what He said, and what He did. They are sung in the hymn "O Come, O Come Emmanuel" and have been used by Christians for around thirteen hundred years!

O Antiphon Traditions

- You can make or buy your own set of O Antiphon ornaments and add one to your Christmas tree each day, starting on December 17.

- Read the Scripture in both the Old and New Testament related to each O Antiphon title.

- Listen to all seven verses of "O Come, O Come Emmanuel" every day during the week leading up to Christmas.

In the final week before Christmas, the O Antiphons help us to renew the focus of Advent. One antiphon is prayed each day and when listed in backwards order, the titles of the O Antiphons spell out EROCRAS—"*ero cras*"—which means "tomorrow, I will come" in Latin.

The O Antiphons are specifically prayed during evening prayer of the Liturgy of the Hours, but they are a beautiful reflection for any type of prayer during the last days of Advent. They tie together Old Testament prophecies and their fulfillment in Christ, asking Jesus to come to us—in Bethlehem, in our hearts, and at the end of time.

Old and New

The O Antiphons make a perfect Advent Bible study. You can use this guide to read more about these titles of Jesus. In the Old Testament passage, you should be looking for promises God made about Who the Messiah would be and what He would do.

In the New Testament passage, you should read for information showing how Jesus fulfilled that prophecy about the Messiah. The passages listed are often very short, so you can also read a little more to understand the context of the passage.

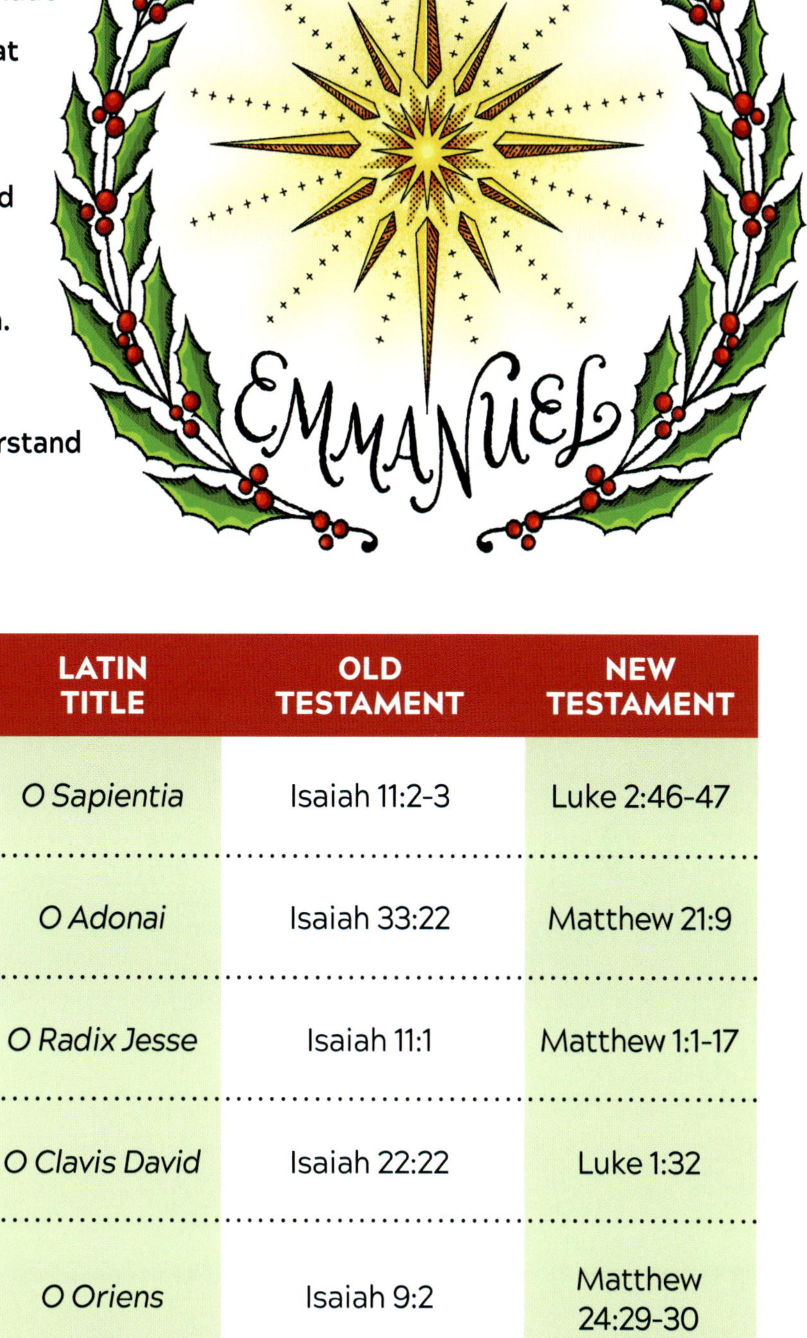

DATE	ENGLISH TITLE	LATIN TITLE	OLD TESTAMENT	NEW TESTAMENT
December 17	O Wisdom	*O Sapientia*	Isaiah 11:2-3	Luke 2:46-47
December 18	O Lord	*O Adonai*	Isaiah 33:22	Matthew 21:9
December 19	O Root of Jesse	*O Radix Jesse*	Isaiah 11:1	Matthew 1:1-17
December 20	O Key of David	*O Clavis David*	Isaiah 22:22	Luke 1:32
December 21	O Radiant Dawn	*O Oriens*	Isaiah 9:2	Matthew 24:29-30
December 22	O King of All Nations	*O Rex Gentium*	Isaiah 9:6	Luke 1:33
December 23	O God Is With Us	*O Emmanuel*	Isaiah 7:14	Matthew 1:22-23

THE LIGHT *of the* WORLD

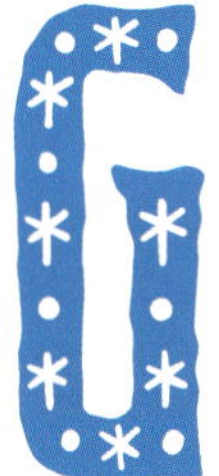

"This is the message we have heard from him and proclaim to you, that God is light and in him is no darkness at all."

— I JOHN 1:5

God has always used light to help us come to know Him. At the creation of the world, God spoke light into being and created the sun, moon, and stars.

Throughout the Old Testament, God is made present to His people through fire and light, like in the burning bush and the pillar of fire in the desert.

The prophet Isaiah said that there would be a day when our light would come, and the glory of the Lord would rise around us (Isa 60:1).

The Book of Revelation tells us that in heaven "night shall be no more; they need no light of lamp or sun, for the Lord God will be their light, and they shall reign for ever and ever" (Rev 22:5).

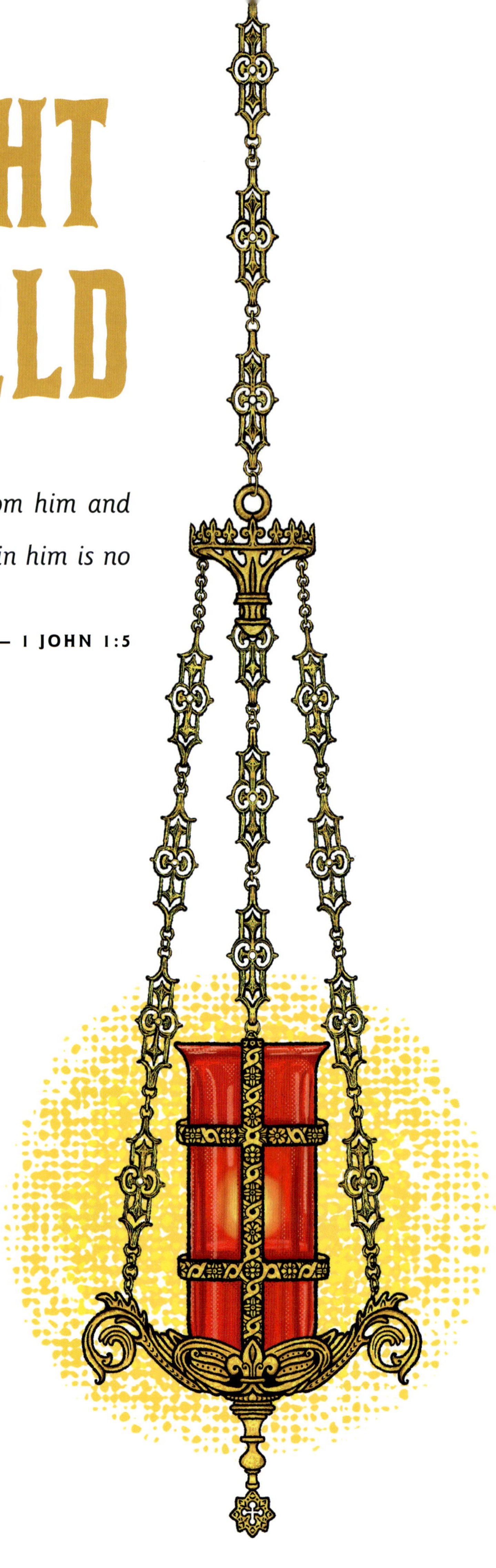

od also used light to announce the birth of His Son, Jesus. On the first Christmas, one of the stars in the sky was called by the Father in heaven to shine brighter than all the rest. The light of that star guided those with open hearts to the gift in the manger. Angels, shepherds, and magi were all led to adore Him by its light.

Jesus would light up the darkness by forgiving our sins. One day He would teach His followers, "I am the light of the world; he who follows me will not walk in darkness, but will have the light of life" (John 8:12).

Jesus, the Messiah and Savior of the world, has come!

OPEN THE SCRIPTURES

"The sun shall no longer be your light by day, nor for brightness shall the moon give light to you by night; but the LORD will be your everlasting light, and your God will be your glory. Your sun shall no more go down, nor your moon withdraw itself; for the LORD will be your everlasting light, and your days of mourning shall be ended."

— ISAIAH 60:19-20

The NATIVITY

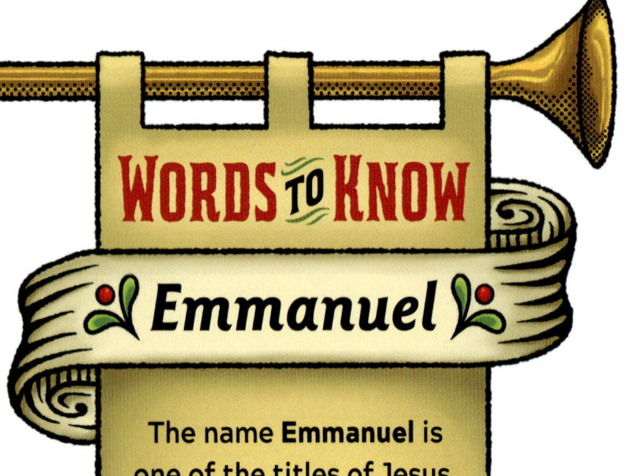

The name Emmanuel is one of the titles of Jesus. It means "God is with us." The prophet Isaiah first foretold that God would come to dwell with His people in Isaiah 7:10-14, and that prophecy is repeated in the Gospel of Matthew 1:22-23.

Jesus is still with us, in every time and in every place. One of the greatest gifts given to the Church is the Holy Eucharist. Jesus is truly with us in the Eucharist that we receive at Mass.

God keeps all of His promises. But sometimes they are fulfilled in a surprising way. The Jewish people likely expected the Messiah would be a conquering king or a ruling hero, but instead He arrived as a tiny baby.

While Joseph and Mary were away from home in the town of Bethlehem the time came for Jesus to be born. Bethlehem was so full of travelers that there was no room for the Holy Family at an inn, but instead they found shelter in a stable with the animals.

The God of the entire universe—all powerful and all knowing—who exists outside of space and time, came to dwell among us in such humble and simple surroundings. The infant Jesus, wrapped tight in swaddling clothes and too weak to walk or even lift His own head, would save the world from sin and open the gates to heaven.

"He who was the Son of God became the Son of man, that man, having been taken into the Word, and receiving the adoption, might become the son of God."

— ST. IRENAEUS[5]

Mary and Joseph weren't alone in their celebration of His birth. In the fields outside of Bethlehem angels sang a glorious song to announce to the shepherds that the Savior had come. They rushed to see Christ and worshiped Him in the stable.

Magi from the East had been watching the sky and they followed a star, traveling from hundreds of miles away to meet the newborn King of the Jews. They brought gifts to lay at His feet, and Mary and Joseph happily welcomed them. From the simple shepherds to the wise magi, Jesus Christ came to save all people.

He came for you and me!

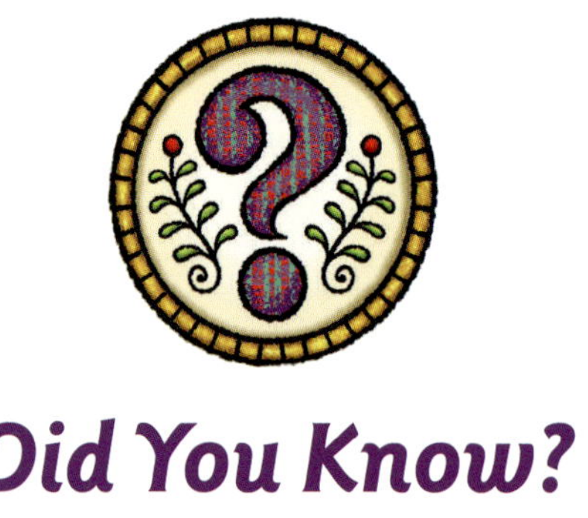

Did You Know?

Did you know that Christmas isn't over in a day? Major feasts in the Church receive an entire Octave, or eight days, of celebration. The Octave of Christmas begins with Christmas Day and continues until January 1. On that day we celebrate the Solemnity of Mary, Mother of God.

Christmas Day is just the beginning! We celebrate the whole Christmas season and carry the wonder of the Incarnation with us all through the year.

While Advent is a season of peaceful hope, expectation, and waiting, Christmas is a time to rejoice that God keeps all of His promises. He is who He says He is, and He does what He says He will do.

Celebrating Epiphany

The Christmas season continues until Epiphany, the visit of the magi, which is celebrated on January 6. The magi (or wise men) traveled far to worship Jesus and brought Him three gifts; gold, frankincense, and myrrh. The gold was for Jesus because He is the King of kings, the frankincense was because He is the great High Priest, and the myrrh was for the sacrifice He would make on the Cross.

The gifts of the wise men are one of the reasons that it is a tradition for family and friends to exchange gifts during the Christmas season. In some cultures, gifts are exchanged on Epiphany instead of Christmas Day.

It also is customary to bless your home on Epiphany, remembering the way that the Holy Family opened their dwelling place to these visitors. You can read the story of the magi in Matthew 2:1-12.

Hidden Symbols at the Nativity

Jesus's mission didn't end at Bethlehem. He came to suffer and die and rise again so that we could have new life. Many details of the Nativity point to the events that would happen years later during Holy Week. Have you ever noticed these hidden symbols?

- Bethlehem means "House of Bread"; Jesus is the Bread of Life

- A manger is a feeding place; Jesus gives us Himself to eat in the Eucharist

- A donkey carried Mary; Jesus rides a donkey into Jerusalem on Palm Sunday

- The infant Jesus was wrapped in cloths just like the cloths used for binding lambs for sacrifice; Jesus is the Lamb of God

- The lantern that Joseph carried is like the sanctuary lamp near the tabernacle

- The swaddling cloths of babies are similar to the burial cloths that bound Jesus in the tomb on Holy Saturday

- St. Joseph cares for and provides a place for Jesus; Joseph of Arimathea provides the new tomb for Jesus's burial

- The gift of myrrh from the wise men is like the burial spices brought by Mary Magdalene to anoint Jesus's body after His death

- Jesus was born in a simple stable and buried in a simple tomb

- The shepherds and the magi (Jews and Gentiles) came to meet Jesus; Jesus came to save all people, both Jews and Gentiles

- The light of the star that guided people to find Jesus is like the sunrise on Easter morning

GOOD NEWS *of* GREAT JOY!

A Christmas Prayer

In the name of the Father, and of the Son, and of the Holy Spirit. Amen.

Jesus, Our Emmanuel, thank you for coming to be with us.

With the angels may we glorify God, praising Him who is so generous and good to us.

With the shepherds may we rush to share the good news that the Messiah has come.

With the magi may we travel a new path, letting our lives be changed by meeting Christ.

With John the Baptist may we prepare the way for the Lord to be known in the world.

With Joseph may we be ready to welcome the Holy Family into our homes.

With Mary may we keep our eyes on the face of Jesus, letting His radiant light shine on us.

With all the saints may we accept the gift of our salvation
and rejoice together in heaven one day.

Jesus, let the love that we feel this Christmas fill every day of the year,
transforming our hearts to be more and more like yours. Amen.

In the name of the Father, and of the Son, and of the Holy Spirit.

Amen.

SOURCES

1. Pope John Paul II, Angelus of Sunday, December 2, 2001, https://www.vatican.va/content/john-paul-ii/en/angelus/2001/documents/hf_jp-ii_ang_20011202.html.

2. Teresa of Calcutta, *Love, a Fruit Always in Season: Daily Meditations from the Words of Mother Teresa of Calcutta,* ed. Dorothy S. Hunt (San Francisco: Ignatius Press, 1987), 32.

3. Fulton J. Sheen, *The World's First Love,* 2nd. ed. (San Francisco: Ignatius Press, 2010), 36.

4. Pope Benedict XVI, Message for Lent 2013, October 15, 2012, https://www.vatican.va/content/benedict-xvi/en/messages/lent/documents/hf_ben-xvi_mes_20121015_lent-2013.html.

5. Irenaeus, *Adversus haereses* 3.19.1, in Ante-Nicene Fathers, vol. 1, trans. Alexander Roberts and William Rambaut, ed. Alexander Roberts, James Donaldson, and A. Cleveland Coxe (Buffalo, NY: Christian Literature Publishing Co., 1885). Revised and edited for New Advent by Kevin Knight, http://www.newadvent.org/fathers/0103319.htm.